ZOMBIES!

A Creepy Coloring Book for the Coming Global Apocalypse

Juscelino Neco

GALLERY BOOKS

New York London Toronto Sydney New Delhi

G

Gallery Books

An Imprint of Simon & Schuster, Inc.

1230 Avenue of the Americas

New York, NY 10020

First/This Gallery Books trade paperback edition June 2016

GALLERY BOOKS and colophon are registered trademarks of Simon & Schuster, Inc.

For information about special discounts for bulk purchases, please contact Simon & Schuster Special Sales at 1-866-506-1949 or business@simonandschuster.com

The Simon & Schuster Speakers Bureau can bring authors to your live event. For more information or to book an event contact the Simon & Schuster Speakers Bureau at 1-866-248-3049 or visit our website at www.simonspeakers.com.

Manufactured in the United States of America

1   3   5   7   9   10   8   6   4   2

Library of Congress Cataloging-in-Publication Data is available.

ISBN 978-1-5011-4405-9

ZOMBIES!

Michael was the tallest of the team. Or he was, until falling from the eighth floor.

In space, no one heard
Harry scream and bite
the helmet's faceplate.

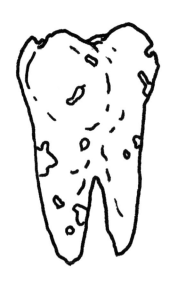

Brooke finally reached
her dream weight.

George was 98% sure he
was going to survive the
zombie apocalypse.

Good food always
brings people closer
to each other.

Alfred hated B-movies.

Tony loves a good beat.

Jake dropped it all to grow wild mulberries and catch up on his reading, having never gotten past page 15 of *Ulysses*.

El Bronco's mom made a vow with
Our Lady of Guadalupe. Even so,
her son didn't quit
the *lucha*.

Steven crapped his pants about getting bald. No more worries.

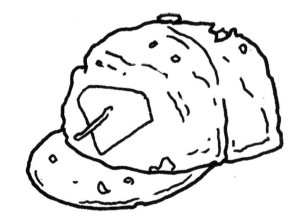

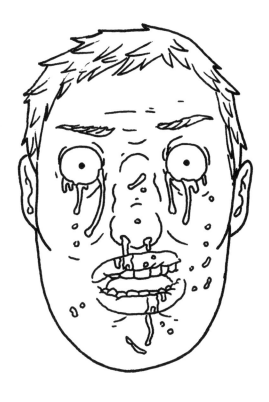
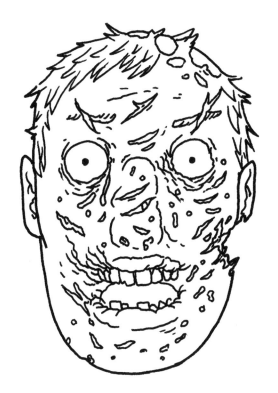

Edgar used to complain
about not having time to
get closer to nature.

When the contagion
started, Yuki decided to put
an end to his life—but he's
still hanging around.

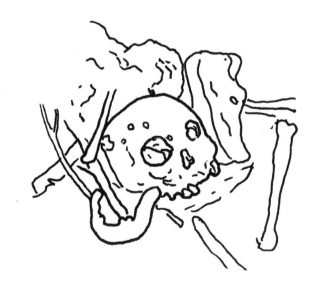

Thomas was always known for
his eloquence.

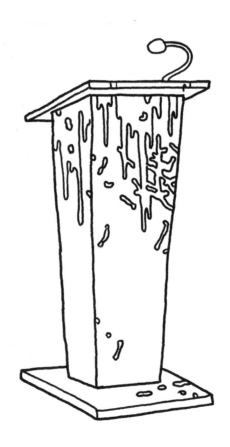

Dry air is terrible for the skin.

Sharon has never read
Edgar Allan Poe.

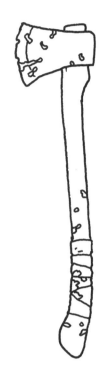

Five heads are better
than one.

Edward thought the circus
was an endless adventure.

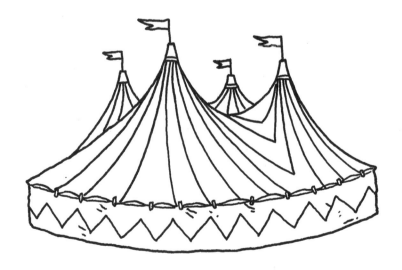

Peter had the neighborhood's most
adorable garden.

Nuclear energy is safe
and efficient.

Bruce never cared about
losing his teeth.

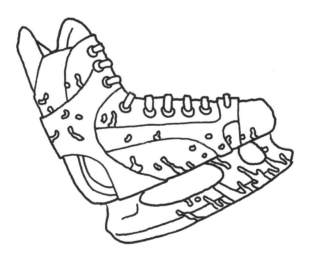

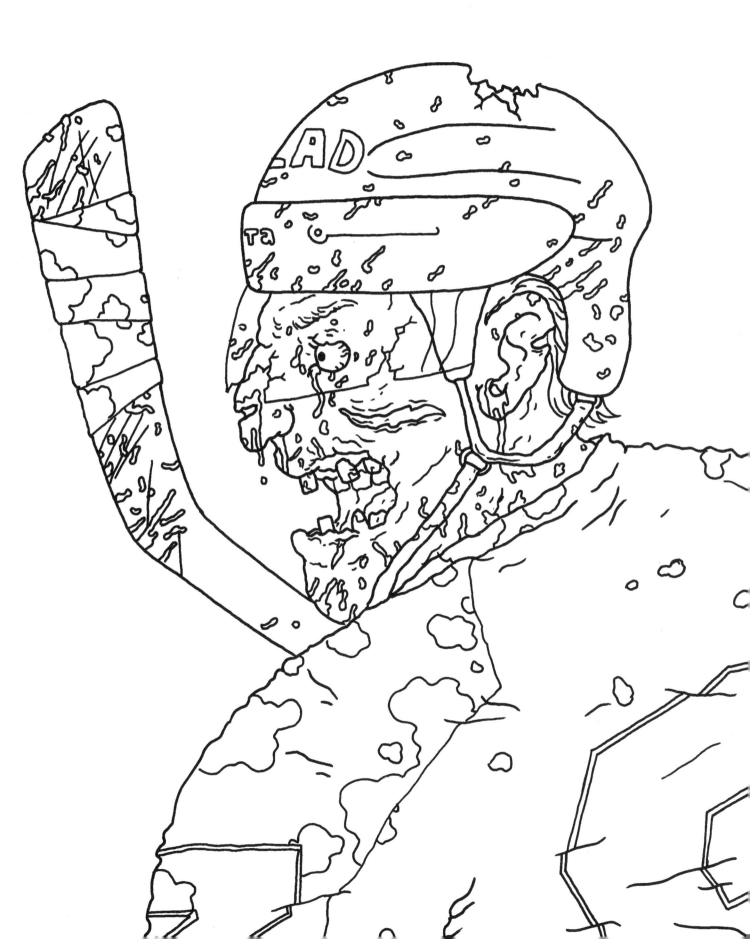

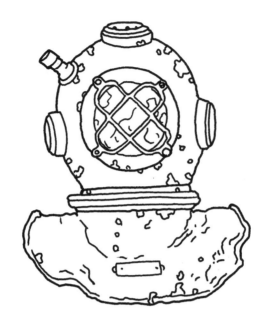

Woody loved a nice
morning swim.

Akira would rather have a
burger than sashimi.

Over the last couple of years,
Ellen spent eighty thousand dollars
on surgeries.

John used to think scurvy was
the worst part of a sea trip.

Jeremiah practiced his guitar day
and night since he was
ten years old.

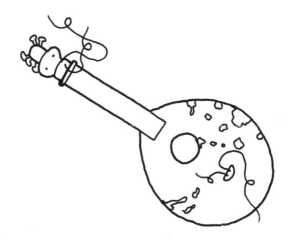

To be a clown, one
must be gifted.

The cold doesn't matter if you're
wearing the right clothes
(or if you're dead,
of course).

Rick has been the manager
of a vegan deli for the
last nineteen years.

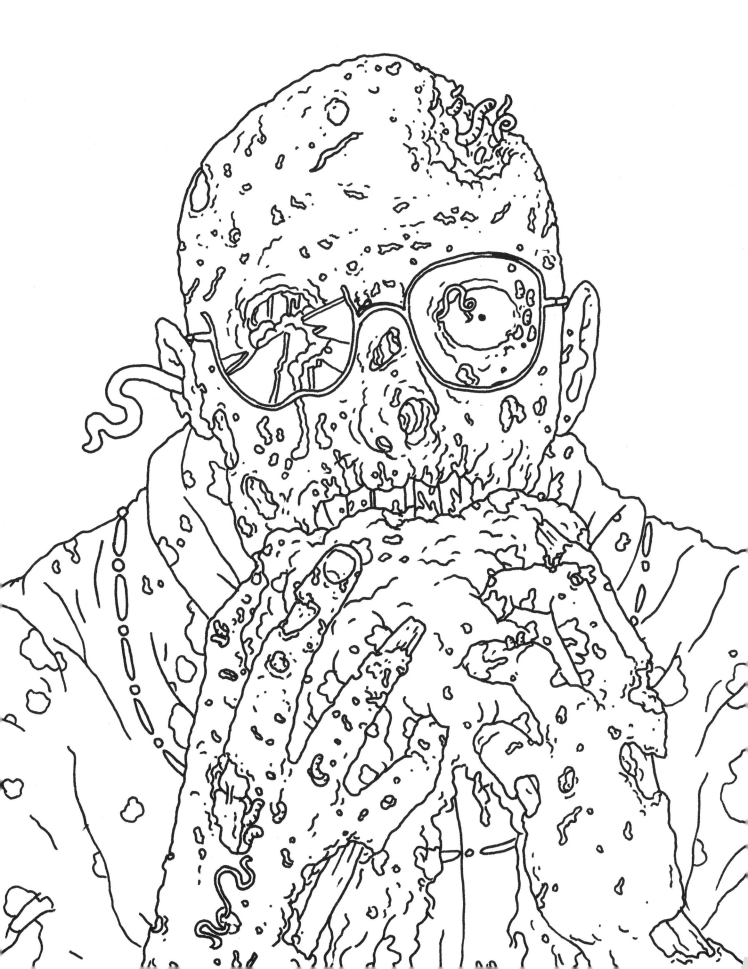

Martha and Daniel have
had a real bond since
high school.

Clarice has never had
acne in her life.